Growin

Polly S

Growing Places

Polly Stretton
Edited by Black Pear Press

First published in 2021 by Black Pear Press
www.blackpear.net
Copyright © Polly Stretton
All rights reserved.

ISBN 978-1-913418-11-3

Cover Photograph and Design by Black Pear Press

Black Pear Press

To Angie—friendship, love, and support

Introduction

This collection of poems is in a sequence covering places where I grew...it brings together memories of childhood and other places both real and imaginary where the process of growing thankfully continues.

My gratitude to everyone who read, commented and supported me when I was selecting poems for this collection. Turning the idea for a poetry collection into a book is as hard as it sounds; it's both challenging and revealing. Thanks to everyone who helped make this happen: Mike Alma, Charley Barnes, Amanda Bonnick, Brian Comber, Nigel Kent, Nina Lewis, Io Osborn, Julia Sandy, and others too numerous to mention. But I shall mention the team at Black Pear Press, always supportive, my sincere thanks.

Other Black Pear Press publications by Polly Stretton:
Girl's Got Rhythm (2012 and 2016)
ISBN 978-1-910322-32-1
Chatterton (2014)
ISBN 978-1-910322-34-5
Four pamphlets, anthologies collated and edited by Polly Stretton commemorating WWI:
   Remembering the Somme (2016) ISBN 978-1-910322-43-7
   The Unremembered of WWI (2017) ISBN 978-1-910322-65-9
   The Unremembered—World War One's Army of Workers—The British Story (2018) ISBN 978-1-910322-84-0
   Motherhood, Loss and the First World War (2018)
   ISBN 978-1-910322-87-1
Pressed Flowers (2019) a poetry anthology curated by Charley Barnes and Polly Stretton
ISBN 978-1-913418-05-2
The Alchemy of 42 (2020)
ISBN 978-1-913418-21-2

Contents

Malvern

not sorry yet

four-year-old legs pumping running away
ma shouts after me 'come back' sister wails
ma is livid i pushed the bowl downstairs
this is how she sees it it is my fault
a tall ten-pint goldfish bowl three goldfish
i run down the meadow behind our house
it is hay-making time yellow grass scent
and dust tickle my nose and make me sneeze
sneeze stops me for long enough she catches
me i have glanced behind in my run and
seen her struggling with my little sister
but ma is grim-faced and determined that
i will be caught and punished it was an
accident i tripped knocked into the bowl
which bounced down each stair fish flying water
arcing the finest mirrored droplets splash
the sound of breaking glass tinkles downwards
she comes out of the kitchen babe on hip
and roars 'nooooo' i flee out the open door
my legs pump i feel my heart i hear my
breath coming jagged i smell the hay i
sneeze she catches me she screams thrashes me
and at each step thrashes me again and again
all up the meadow back into the house
she is crying hot angry tears
me howling
mortified indignant rebellious
an accident i sob my jaw jutting
i am four-years-old
not sorry yet

'Don't Swing on the Railings'

Worcester Royal Infirmary steps,
in Castle Street,
found me waiting, aged five,
for Pa to come home.
We didn't go into the hospital.
I didn't know why.

I wore a blue velvet-collared coat,
Ma, her mulberry cloche hat.
I stroked my soft collar
until Ma made me stop.

Pa had been poorly,
lived on eggs and milk for months,
I loved the sugary eggs and milk
—still smell the mix.
Ma made it in a Horlicks maker,
a glass jar and a plunger with holes.
She would work it up and down,
up and down, until it frothed.
Ma said it was all he could keep down;
I didn't know what that meant.

I wasn't allowed to sit on the steps,
so held onto the cold iron railing
with the chipped black paint. I ran
my other hand across the surface: pitted,
pocked, rough yet smooth.
There were bits of blue
under the black.
         'Don't swing on the railings,' Ma said.
She didn't say why.

I counted the red bricks,
there were nine between the cream blocks.
I counted them.   contd...

2

I could count up to ten.

When Pa came out
he knocked Ma's hat off
—accidentally—
she tutted but smiled.
I didn't know why.

Candles and Splinters

The fruit is stacked
on racks Father made:
wooden, tough, splintery, like Mother.

The cellar doors creak,
a cast latch speaks with a clatter
as the doors shut fast.

My hands search for matches, forbidden matches,
and candles, forbidden candles,
a saucer to catch the wax.

The scent of sweet apples
gift-wrapped in old newspaper,
blends with the tang of lit tapers.

I breathe claggy coal dust,
a crack of light gusts.
I'm behind a column,
shielding the candle,
my lips purse.

The latch catch shakes,
my heart palpates,
a dozen steps down
from the sliver of a frown
on the brow of a peevish mother;

her ire pares a path towards me.

What Ma Said

I heard Ma say...
I heard Ma say,
she had to rob Peter
to pay Paul today,
'cos us kids wanted
a bob or two,
to pay for milk
when we got to school.
She thrust hair back
from her creased-up brow,
looked round to see me
said, 'Get going now.'
The catch in her voice
haunts me still,
her soft-spoken words,
I see her tears well,
'cos she wept when she said,
'You haven't a clue,'
and added an onion
to rabbit stew.

Walk

After church we walk
the country lanes.
Just us—and Ma—Pa's working.
My little sister,
    blonde curls bobbing,
Ma, unseeing, frozen,
lips tight on some imagined slight.

Three rose-clambered dresses
that appeared in the local paper,
at a show where we plunged our arms
into nose itching sawdust
for gifts in blue or pink tissue.
    'Smile for the camera'.
'My girls,' Pa says, face beaming, eyes as blue as my
sister's,
while my eyes, as dark as hers are pale,
brood on the whimsical ribbon-bows
precise on side-partings above her pretty face,
though mine scowls.

We come to the tree, the side-on tree,
we cannot climb it in our roses,
it's implicitly forbidden
    in Ma's straight back, determined stride.
I long to cling onto the low-slung trunk,
into arms that hug me.

Ma makes headway. I must catch up or risk
a scolding as severe as salt.
Close-mouthed, buttoned-up, mum,
she looks back, and I, suffocated,
abandon the tree
and walk.

Yellow Dusters

Pa, a signalman,
tells of drawers
full of yellow dusters.

Enter the signal box,
s *k* *i* *d*
on two red-edged yellow dusters,
blanket stitched around four sides,
placed so you could skid
s *k* *i* *d*
along the chestnut brown polished floor
the cloths under your feet,
you teeter—you almost fall.

The scent of the box,
oil warm on railway levers,
polish and blacking for the range,
beeswax for the floors,
the signal box shines mirror bright.

I always imagined
I'd been born
in a drawer full of yellow dusters.

Her Girls

We do not share blood,
we share memories.
A lifetime of growing together
with the closest of parents.
We ran running races, you always behind me
egging me on.
You refused to go to ballet, I missed you.
I had to take you everywhere,
my little stalker,
even on my first date,
a trip to the cinema,
he cancelled because you were there.
You, bashing me with a Scholl sandal
by the coal bunker,
made brave by the presence of your friend
and Pixie the dog.
Dancing at local discos,
practising eyeliner, shadow, mascara
until Pa said, "Take that muck off your face."
Sharing scents: 'Californian Poppy'
and one with 'Paris' in its name
in a silver-topped blue bottle
bought from Woolworths.
Pinching Ma's 'Mum' stick deodorant
that made honeyed soft stains
on her girls.
Ma saying you needed a bra
more than me, even though
you were two years younger.
We were at Burnham-on-Sea
—the hottest, burniest
holiday ever—
Nivea suntan lotioned
we stretched on the sands, hand-in-hand.

Re Cycling

I have cycled for miles delivering newspapers.
I've braved barking, snarling,
snapping dogs and made friends,
learned to hold open unknown letterboxes
to avoid chopped-off digits,
crunched gravel drives
and 'come in for a cuppa' near the end of the round.
I have suffered frozen black fingers,
welcomed new babies,
cried over losses.
I've been first with the news.
I know the route,
when to coast,
when to peddle like fury;
enjoyed the whish of rubber tyres in the sun,
the fog, rain, sleet and snow.
I've learned how to slide
and skid my bike to a stop;
repaired punctures,
pumped countless tyres
and had a sore bum from bouncing
down steps.
I have a knack of knowing
which day will be heavy
with comics and mags.
My canvas bag has 'Daily Mirror'
stamped in red and cream.
I've sturdy shoes and a quilted black coat.

I have cycled for miles delivering newspapers.
I still have all my fingers.

The Making

You watch me a while,
fascinated by the up
down silver flash,
blinking at the clatter dash
of levers and pulleys;
wheel circling,
my foot depressed
to create,
whirring away.
Now you play
with reels building
a tower or making a snake.
Your brothers, all rough
and tumble, disrupt
specks of cotton.
The snake becomes
a chuffing train
circling the lino at speed
until they break
the carriages from the engine,
worth nothing, no heed.
They go, to leave
just you with me
again, as I cut,
shape, and start to finish
—whirr,
whirr, whirr—

Familiar Palms

I meet him halfway,
in a café
between his home and mine.

My heart rails,
impaled, yet veiled.

We walk slowly—at first—
then we run
—overwhelmed—together.

He wears a worsted jacket,
rough, sweet-smelling

he hugs me close
like we've known each other always.

Inside the café, we can't stop,
can't stop talking
—talking—

I notice his hands,
his hands.

I take his in my own,
turn it palm upwards
—mine too—

there's no doubt:
carbon copies.

Father and daughter,
meet at last.

Lines revealed. Hearts unveiled.
All in the palms of our hands.

Malvern Hills

Swifts

Silence and solitude unbroken drops
a sense of stillness, soundlessness flutters,
no soul to disturb the cool, calm hilltop,
Midsummer Hill smothers sighs, hushed, shuttered.
And then from the West come the saucy swifts,
swooping and singing, playing today, while
they wait to migrate, chase, drift, flit and lift,
wings skitter, dip and dance to the sundial.
What joy in aloneness, how glad the sight,
a ballet of darting, diving divas
so rare, a flock of sure swifts in full flight,
they plunge, lunge and soar in joie de vivre.
    There's none to disturb the cool, calm hilltop,
    Midsummer Hill sighs in silence, shuttered.

Raw

I think of feet tramping and treading waved hills,
of stories, songs and poems stone tracks inspire,
of creatures great and small that shout and trill,
of men, myths of monsters, faeries, giants.
A million years and more, they've stood to brood;
a vale eruption, ridgebacked, raw and proud,
they beckon, call upon us to intrude,
and haunting bluebell oceans trumpet loud.
Yet when I climb those taxing slopes once more,
to see the valleys spread out far below,
I will be searching for an ancient shore,
that seeing through a spyglass cannot show,
    The light and shade illuminated when
      my eyes are dim and I shan't come again.

Spring

Banish the blues with a red touch;
blend them purple for tomorrow,
boys and clinker don't mean too much
warm debris for the wheelbarrow.
Pigeons perch on the old scarecrow,
who imagines lilacs in spring,
they watch the boy make a furrow
and prepare for life on the wing.

Echoes

In the present, from the past,
voices echo
sayings last
even when the body has gone,
what was said will linger on.
'My mum used to say...'
'My grannie too...'
'My dad would have something to say to you.'
In the present, from the past,
voices echo,
echoes last.

Moonlight in Jars

On the Malverns
under the stars
where faerie folk catch
moonlight in jars
along Shire Ditch
for the jaded witch
and only the brave
pass the giant's cave
where rock and loam
say nothing of home
say something of home
say all about home

Capability | The Reason

You're more capable,
more sensible,
more able to get by.
You'll go and make a life for yourself,
she'd sit at home and cry.

Worcester

I love lychgates—those structures at the entrance of some churches that brides like to be photographed beneath—there are many such churches in Worcestershire. This led to me looking into their history. At the same time, I was fascinated by the poetry form of the Kyrielle, based on the Kyrie. This poem is the outcome.

Beyond the Veil

Handkerchiefs, white twisted prayer,
sobs breach and break the mourning air,
death takes, will not be second-guessed,
a shroud beneath the lychgate rests.

The shelter with its angled roof
hears clattering of horses' hooves,
covers the dear departed, blessed;
her shroud beneath the lychgate rests.

The bearers seated by the corpse
know flesh, bones, come to nothing, naught
to ponder, but in time accept,
a shroud beneath the lychgate rests.

From lych to church seems overlong,
they pause, they pray, they chant their song,
to see her pass this way—none guessed
a shroud around the lych would rest.

A hot ague shook her life away,
the children sobbed, begged her to stay,
but death took life, imbibed her breath,
a shroud beneath the lychgate rests.

Yet that was then, and this is now,
time changes, untracked: marriage vow,
photo backdrop, bride with guests,
a shroud beneath the lychgate rests.

contd...

Spectres, spirits of the passed,
plague actors in the wedding cast,
this shady place does it oppress
if shrouds beneath the lychgate rest?

'Death is the only deathless one',[1]
time lingers brief, they've just begun,
this is for life, no trial or test,
a shroud beneath the lychgate rests.

Fading out the nuptial glitter,
shadows cast by bygone sitters,
carnation wilts upon his breast,
and shrouds beneath the lychgate rest.

The charm of years, a pretty place.
He gazes down on her sweet face.
Craves togetherness, wedded, yes.
A shroud beneath the lychgate rests.

Farewell
In memory of Tana Durham

I see you in the sky blossoms:
lapis lazuli, pearls of clouds;
in laburnum chains,
lime links and leafy shrouds.
And the sunshine's silverfish show.

Think of days like today
when the sun shines because it can.
I remember you, my friend,
and the times we mis-spent
together.

---

[1] From *Kyrielle* by John Payne (1842–1916)

Hobgoblin Trees

See the way the shadows flee
from a frame turned to the sun.
Arms outstretched, hobgoblin trees
reach for skies soul-darkened breeze.

Spring will come as come it may,
frost pale icicles undone
see the way the shadows pray,
anemones bloom every day.

Arms outstretched, hobgoblin trees,
battered now by wind and sun,
lengthened in the seasoned trees,
see the way the shadows tease.

Water stretches wild as bees,
frozen edge tiptoes outrun,
arms outstretched, hobgoblin trees,
emboss old frost's chill-white chemise.

See the depths old frost decrees
with his face turned to the sun,
see the way his shadow flees,
arms outstretched, hobgoblin trees.

Gull over the Flood

You don't see me at first,
but I am here.
My maw gapes, the wind rushes
colourless, obtuse, rank with rot,
dries my open throat;
I shriek with rage; you hear me.
I will not be unheard.
I dive for detritus,
tearing your eardrums.
Your rubbish, your litter: my food.
Air buffets, plucking feathers that pirouette
and fade as they fly away.
I dive into decay,
water: the flood.

Waves thrash, boil brown mud, white spume.
My ancient oak perch is stranded
deep in wetlands, the Powick Hams,
it grows taller yet looks smaller,
stands steadfast as a sentry,
the torrent sloshes, surrounds its trunk.
I splash, struggle against the surge,
am sodden, water-heavy.
I settle on burnt chemical mix,
snatch at flapping bags, shred red plastic,
rainwater drips, drenches; I scream in fury;
you hear me.
Malvern Hills yawn,
they've seen it all before.

I'm a troublesome tittle-tattle on rising tides,
I sign and signal on roofs, on telegraph poles,
wherever I land.

contd…

A trance of superstition, the rattle of rough voice
distanced by ruffling winds
that brings another spate.
I stretch my throat
and reach for the roiling skies,
advance,
then, wanting the wind in my mouth again,
dip into the deluge,
I swoop, I screech,
I wave, but do not drown.

Acid Velvet

I stroll gravelled paths
at my first flower show,
zesty lime masses soft in the sun:
Nicotiana alata.
Salver-shaped leaves
wave in the breeze, utter
in the border,
a flutter of inflorescent flora,
tobacco panicles
of a younger summer.

Acid velvet trumpets throw
a twilight scent;
chime of colour beloved
in city and courtyard,
fragrance pours for moths
who mutter in cottage gardens.
And I, at my first flower show,
fall in love with Solanaceae
and its toxic charms,
for life.

'Letter Writing in the Moonlight' and 'Pale Horse' were written for the Worcestershire Poet Laureate Nina Lewis's (2017) project 'A Tale of Two Cities' in which Worcester UK poets were matched with Worcester USA poets and created 'call and response' poems.

Letter Writing in the Moonlight

Beneath the apple tree
all is still.
Night, as dark as her lover,
veils the lush grass;
bramble and thistle
scratch, inscribe the ground.

A mist hovers,
loathe to leave the river,
low down in the depths of the garden
where mud oozes
and the odour of damp
settles.

The bench is warm,
as graffitied as her heart.
Love holds her
like the mist—all pervasive—
toads and crickets mock,
'Write'.

A moonbeam strikes
through cloud.
Clouds steal onwards
and soon the lawn
is shown in a puddle of silver light.
She puts pen to paper.

Pale Horse

Heels down. Head up. Look
where you're going.
Go to a place
where you can hear your heart;
listen to the beat,
forget the drub of a thousand pale hooves
and the horsemen of the apocalypse.
We rise and fall together.

Grandma had a penny to remember you,
a bronze memory she Brassoed weekly,
cast in physical prowess, spiritual power,
in devotion to the triumph of good,
Britannia faces left, holds a laurel wreath,
there's a box beneath, holding your name in raised relief,
and you, a man of miracles.
We rise and fall together.

A circular coin made whole, inscribed:
'He died for freedom and honour'.
You are a man who has gone,
yet nonetheless lives.
Your Penelope still waits.
Put the littered marshy slew behind you,
put it behind you.
We rise and fall together.

Go to a place
where you can hear your heart;
listen to the beat.
No pale horse snickers,
no harbinger rides quicker,
no more horseshoes, trench fever, heat.
We sleep.
We rise and fall together.

Crown East

Latent

Grey, receding,
the fragrance of his shaving gel.
He carries an iPad.
The first thing to leave
is the light of his eyes.
I touch his absence;
a disembodied voice,   'see you later.'
There are magical contortions
made by the dust,
they swirl in the sunbeams that
pour through the east window,
and echo, 'later, later.'
I still feel the tweed jacket,
rough against my fingers,
it lingers with his shadow in the room.

Dream On

I dream of the day I'll have a home:
thatched; rose scent round the door,
an illusion, a tree-sheltered lane,
with a legendary path of loam
that leads to a spectral seashore
where cool clean wraiths of white foam
are as silk beneath bare feet.

*A 'Little Poem' for World Poetry Day organised by Worcestershire Poet
Laureate Nina Lewis (2017)*

Bittersweet

I see him
walking with his children
at the funfair.
A light day, a spritely day,
a visionary, unsightly day.

I follow,
heaving through the crowds,
breathless,
deathless,
desperate
to exhale what's left
and speak to him.

One frantic romantic.

As I draw closer
it is clear
—severe—
as the day chilled,
my throat angst-filled,
it isn't him.

I fold in upon myself.

Bones Under a Bridge

Tiny pile of bones
under a bridge
you were found out;
talked to the hawk,
or a murder of crows.

Maybe your first love,
the one that found you
in flagrante
set you up,
or the second, the witness,
who heard your infidelity.

Selfish, you will be alone.
The bridge won't help.
We celebrate
bones beneath the bridge.
You always said,
'No one cares.'

If You Didn't Get This Message, Call Me

No answer,
no reply,
no phone call,
no email,
no text
or other messages.

No chocolates,
no flowers,
no pretty negligee,
no PJs;
nobody in,
no one out.

No one at home,
no heart,
no thing.

The Banished Ash | Yggdrasill

'Yggdrasill[2] shivers,
the ash, as it stands.
The old tree groans...[3]'
and, only now, we're 'ready to go'?

Our Anglo-Saxon heritage hails
ash spears, shield-handles,
smooth, strong, tough,
flexible ash: walking sticks; tent pegs;
oars; hurleys; gates; tool handles; wheel rims;
aircraft wings
for the De Havilland Mosquito in World War II.

In the olden days naked children
passed through the split trunk of ash
in a ritual to cure: heal rickets.

Chalara Fraxinea infects,
displays diamond lesions,
rampant in Europe,
rife in East Anglian woods.
Repeat Dutch elm disease,
repeat the scourge of the 70's—
repeat.

The elm recovers,
yet is not as common
as once-upon-a-time.
Act faster!

contd…

---

[2] *pr: igdrasil*
[3] *Völuspá* (Poetic Edda, 13th century)
http://www.bbc.co.uk/news/science-environment-20176720
http://www.forestry.gov.uk/chalara

Save our woods!
Fend off fungus,
fight for borrowed forests.

'Yggdrasill shivers,
the ash, as it stands.
The old tree groans...[4]'
Mould attacks.
Ash dieback.
And, only now, we're 'ready to go'?

They knew about it.

---

[4] *Völuspá* (Poetic Edda, 13th century)
http://www.bbc.co.uk/news/science-environment-20176720
http://www.forestry.gov.uk/chalara

Croome Court

'William's Footprint' refers to William Dean, who arrived at Croome in about 1796 and was Head Gardener to the 6th and 7th Earls of Coventry for nearly 40 years looking after the walled kitchen garden and the park. He wrote a book about Croome and indexed every plant and tree.

William's Footprint

If soles could talk
what tales they'd tell
of statues—alive!—
hot walls and wishing wells;
of a serpentine river
and a man-made lake,
of Quercus ilex
and poison mandrake.

If soles could talk
what tales they'd tell,
of the walled kitchen garden
and glass cloche bells,
of boys of seven
who stoke the heated wall,
while the dipping pond
is their longed-for call.

If soles could talk
what tales they'd tell,
of the Druid and Sabrina's
trysts in the dell;
of mischievous Pan
piping high and sweet,
the goat-god spies on them
in the grotto where they meet.   contd...

If soles could talk
what tales they'd tell,
of the nymphs of Croome,
wooded islands where they dwell,
and head gardener Will
wielding spade and pruning hook;
spiritually ready
to pen his book.

'A Minuet in Time' is a celebration of the happy family years of Anne Somerset Countess of Coventry—spent at Croome Court. Her time there ended in tragedy, but she lived to a ripe old age. The poem is in a Villanelle form to reflect the Minuet, a dance of the era—and pantables are shoes.

A Minuet in Time

The minuet traces a timely dance,
Anne dips and sways on pantables, shapely.
The Countess quickens to Mozart: enchants.

Silven-thread velvety feet take the chance
to step and twirl with the Earl, as, chastely,
the minuet traces a timely dance.

The night is set soft and clear for romance,
she dances with poise and grace, sedately.
The Countess quickens to Mozart: enchants.

Tom writes, 'My dear Rogue,' and this circumstance
shows his love for her: elegant lady.
The minuet traces a timely dance.

His shoes buckled black, hers, turquoise, advance
soul to sole and sumptuous, stately.
The Countess quickens to Mozart: enchants.

'My Croome Court years of cheer, of jubilance,
'but then the death of my dear family.'
The minuet traces a timely dance.
The Countess quickens to Mozart: enchants.

Four Terms

Four empty corners once held Roman Terms,
there's nothing where splendour, once affirmed,
slipped away for mysterious reasons;
cool, eye-catching Elysian Seasons.

Near Temple Greenhouse, a Lancelot place,
Evergreen Shrubbery in a warm embrace
sees criss-crossed walks, hears insect legs thrumming;
pale plinths await lost statues' homecoming.

Yet cedars of Lebanon fan the park,
while winds whine and winnow, whispering dark,
seeking heads and shoulders vanished from plinths
missed in a moment and mourned ever since.

Olympian gates in fields of flowers
hang on the return of hidden Hours.

Tender Fruit

You must have smelled the plums,
every one I picked.
    They're telling me to pant,
    that you're not ready yet.

You must have felt the ladder
pressed against your silhouette.
    They're telling me to take deep breaths,
    that I'm not ready yet.

Purple plum bloom's soft,
it rubs off to the touch.
    They're telling me to push
    that the pain is 'not too much.'

See the rotten plums fall,
waspy with decay.
    They say that I am bleeding,
    you must be born without delay.

I glimpse your wrinkled face,
hear your lusty cry.
    They say that I am fading,
    fading, fading...

The next two poems relate to the boys who went to 'The Court' properly titled 'St Joseph's School for Boys' at Croome Court 1948-1978.

Questions to Schoolboys

Where did you come from,
where did you go?
Where did you come from,
so long ago?

A home of love and lots of life,
or a place of danger, hate and strife?
Did your past inform the ways
you lived at school,
your work, your play?

Did you think all was the same,
that life had played a wretched game?
Did you know why you were here
in this mansion, full of fear?
Did you love three meals a day?
What if you dared disobey?
Were you thought a tearaway?

Were you beaten?

Where did you come from,
where did you go?
Where did you come from,
so long ago?

Nuns Talking

'Oh those boys,
'oh, those boys,
'full of nonsense,
'full of noise,
'can't they keep their voices down?
'Running round and round and round.'

    'Headmistress, please, do not fret so.
    'They mean no harm, they're young, you know.'

'Sister Ursula, you see no fault
'in any boy doing somersaults
'or stealing cake from the table.
'They must learn
'to kneel, be prayerful.
'Giving them an inch is fatal!'

    'Headmistress, they are but boys
    'they have no home, they have few toys,
    'we are all to them, and more,
    'the minute they walk through our door.'

'Bah! I say, "but boys" indeed,
'all they want is a jolly good feed.
'They don't want to work at all,
'lazy boys who play with balls.
'They should work hard at their studies,
'not play football with their buddies.
'I'm tired of wiping noses, bloodied,
'they come in with their boots all muddied...'

    'Sister, Sister, patience please,
    'there is no harm in bloodied knees,
    'let them have some fun and joy,
    'it is not easy, being a boy.'

Droitwich

'Curves' and 'Folk Like Us | Winds of Change' were written for the Worcestershire Poet Laureate Nina Lewis's (2017) Hanbury Hall project. 'Curves' was selected to be read at the closing of the exhibition—inspired by a red squirrel painted by Chris Walker, the squirrel was sitting on a branch and her shape looked like the letter C.

Curves

She owns it:
the branch.
She's ready for summer
in a lighter coat.
Her curves tell
of coppery kittens
to be born later today,
two, three, or four will arrive
to inhabit the drey.

The painter's sable brush,
pure,
soft as a blush
to define the narrow
smart face in a tuft-eared embrace.
A picture to enhance the repeated romance
of a cheeky red squirrel
in Norfolk.

The artist describes,
in faint, refined strokes,
sharp arched claws
curved in applause,
and a tail, balanced to guide
a talent that tints
the nut connoisseur,
against the bark
and spiky cones of the conifer.

Folk Like Us | Winds of Change

Open waistcoat, tinted glasses,
fat black moustache;
he's willing the teddy-boy
to mend the bike.
1950's Middle England,
post-war, pre-PC; transitions,
pop-music is positioned
to take over the world.

*Inspired by a painting by
Graham Wilson entitled
'Saturday Morning'*

The wind streams fragrant smoke
and waves the washing away...
no sooty sheets today.
Broken fences scatter,
they don't matter
in a jovial terraced scene;
a typical weekend for folk like us.

Mum, pinnied, scarved, lugs the prop,
her girl holds a basket of clothes aloft.
The dog's on alert,
and look, there's Bert
tending his pigeons,
braces crossed,
—Bert never goes out without braces—

The baby hears the wind,
sheets flap, prop scrapes, bike engine stutters,
dog barks, and the boy in the shed
fires his cap-gun. 'BANG'.
It makes baby jump.
Mum—the one with the red hat—
tucks the blankets closer.
The baby's wrapped up snug,
as the winds of change blow.

'Spade', 'Bird on Spade', and 'Head—Alone' were written on The Jinney Ring Sculpture Trail with Worcestershire Poet Laureate Nina Lewis (2017)

Spade

My purpose is to turn soil,
not to act as a perch
for a rust-ridden bird made of scrap
no good for anything else.
My self abhors the chuckles of passers-by,
they don't know what I can handle:
I have toiled; in soil I've turned;
I worked hard yet I was spurned
and then discarded...
now I'm found.

Bird on Spade

I came into being
retrieved from a skip,
chunky, clunky rusted scrap
—thought useless—
a curious bird,
head tilted, perched,
my claws grip a warm wooden handle,
my nuts and bolts shown
to the world.

Head—Alone

I am ancient art or the apocalypse,
I don't see your footsteps
I hear the disturbed gravel.
You breathe your bumbling tones,
wonder if I'm sleeping or dead.
You say I look soft-boiled

I feel your fingertip
bones on my rumpled skin
as if touching parchment
—serenity—
yet...not skin, but limestone

Bees and bugs my bedfellows,
my egg of a head lies alongside
the fragrance of lavender
and fresh,
pitiless,
spikes of grass.

Fantasy Places

Becoming the Sea | Amphitrite

I will tell water vapour to escape
from molten Earth
into the atmosphere;

I'll inhale humidity, mist,
breathe easier.
Let it cool for rain to fall
to my face, smooth on my skin.

I'll insist that it's time,
time for the moon's pull
to create the tidal force, the push,
the pull of Selene

against every other mass;
it begets Earth's bulge
and makes me high tides to dance in,
gives boats breakers to rock,
buoys me up to see starlit skies.

Iris

You are a rainbow, a gilded-winged messenger,
a fresh-faced goddess
refilling rain clouds with seawater.
Speed of the wind,
Zephyrus
by your side.

Plunge
into the ocean, dark underworld,
unhindered by the caduceus,
unchecked before sea serpents.

Harpy sister
bring to Zeus the great oath of gods,
Iris, take him your ewer
sweet syrup of nectar.
Swift-footed, sure, storm-like rage
of the messenger bent on your twin.
Your joy flowing from Arke's wings on Achilles' heels.

Harbinger of light in a gossamer gown:
ruby red;
organza orange;
yarrow yellow;
gecko green;
byzantine blue;
important indigo;
virtuous violet
—the realm of the rainbow is yours—
always beyond reach.

The Vengeful Ghost

She drifts up the stairs filament light
floats down the landing quiet as the night
melts through the door to where her man lies
he'll see her no more through his lying eyes

A chill in the air a breeze past his cheek
his wife has been dead for exactly one week
his heart is heavy lowered like lead
she left him a token in orange and red

He looks at the painting from her hand and head
it's been celebrated its fame has spread
across the land she's a household name
for pictures depicting fire and flame

Paint on her palette brushes and knife
linseed oil scent clung to her in life
and now that smell with its memorable tang
announces she's haunting her faithless man

A fragranced candle glitters and gutters
wisps of black smoke pass and flutter
she does not weep for the life she's lost
she will haunt him loathe him at no cost

She'll set fires to show him what he has done
remember the times they were as one

The demons that drove her to paint fire and flame
now make it easy to come back again
He has the painting orange and red
she has the means and he'll live in dread

Flawless

Flawless has a Wabi[5] and Ostranenie[6] theme

Find the Persian pebble-edged river,
cross the candyfloss bridge
to pure graph paper.
Work a motif, mina-khani, rosette
aching on acanthus
in repeating figures
borrowed from weavers,
and know
there is no more.
Perfection is another's domain.

---

[5] *Wabi means things that are fresh and simple. It denotes quietude and simplicity and combines these attributes with rustic beauty. It includes both the natural world and that which is made by man. It can also mean an unintended or happenstance element, maybe even a small flaw which gives elegance and uniqueness to the whole, such as the pattern made by a flowing glaze on a ceramic object.*

[6] *A neologism, it implies two kinds of actions: making strange, and pushing aside. The concept refers to techniques writers use to transform ordinary language into poetic language which is said to induce a heightened state of perception.*

Question Mark Latch

with acknowledgement to Penelope Lively (Moon Tiger, 1987)

She chooses a ring for their future, for memories within
    memories.
It holds a conical lid on a tiny-hinged box and a question
    mark latch; a complex band for a chronicler.
A poison ring.
It sits heavy on her finger.

She sees sand trickle into the box, grains falling outside,
    discarded.
He bought it in WWII,
presented it, filled it with sand from the Mokkatam Hills.

Years later, her daughter demands the ring,
wants to clean it, empty it of dirt.
Her chill red-faced mother snaps:
    'Put it back where you found it'.

Memories within memories, she a journalist, he a tank
    officer
to be reported missing—confirmed dead.
    'What will you do when the war's over?'

'Keep the dead with me forever;
I shan't climb the Pyramids.'

The Ghost Ship | A Sestina

"Hope" found "The Jenny", the crew frozen dead,
the captain deceased at his log, he'd scribed
in pen and black ink. The written note said,
'No food for seventy-one days,' and he died.
But how, why, when, what was the watershed?
A cryptic chiller: all were mystified.

The ghost ship appeared, they were mystified,
it drifted through spooky mist, sound was dead,
weird shapes, foul smells, a scary watershed.
The final thing the captain did: he scribed,
wrote in his log, and then the poor man died.
'The crew gone, my time has come,' he said.

Ghost ships are abandoned, it's often said,
looming in the bay, sailors mystified,
as to how, why, when and where the men died.
Strange for all aboard to be stone cold dead.
The skipper outlived them, and he had scribed
through the crisis: the unknown watershed.

Ghostly trauma, a mystery watershed.
This was what fishermen on the shore said,
they crossed themselves and muttered, some scribed
like the captain, sea mist left them mystified.
'All dead,' they cried, their skin crawled, 'all are dead.'
They couldn't imagine how they had died.

The mist swirled, the men glanced, shook, 'all died,'
shuddered at the thought of the watershed,
was the ship ice-trapped, did that freeze them dead?
'If so, how did captain live on?' they said.
Sea mist rose, fell, and heard them mystified,
pondering most why the captain had scribed.

contd...

They had no logs, no words to be scribed,
they scratched their heads, why had the captain died?
They found no answer, remained mystified.
Hearts laboured dread about the watershed,
'There's more in heaven and earth,' often said,
'One thing's for sure, they are all dead as dead.'

No one found out how, why and where they died,
'There's no answer, 'tis a ghost ship' they said,
and shaking their heads, remained mystified.

Leave the Tarot

Close the windows,
turn the key,
batten all hatches,
stay in with me.

Shoot the cellar bolt,
lock the French doors,
keep the kitchen safe
—no time for chores—

Padlock the gate
make the dining room secure.
Leave the Tarot cards
in the sideboard drawer.

Don't even think of the Ouija board,
we won't be keeping an account or score.
It's spooky tonight, and I've told you before,
whatever you do...don't open the door.

The Skin of the Selkie
a simple retelling of the myth

Scottish tales told in the flickering flames of fire
tell of maidens dancing in the moonlight.
There are three with black hair, dark shining eyes
and soft olive skin, watched by three brothers.

Pity the selkies, who love to dance in warmth
on the shore. At midnight they discard sealskins
squeeze out from the balmy humidity, scratchy salt,
cast off the sweaty ozone of the cold sea.

They're seaweed slippery—born into the world,
prance on the sands, arms stretched to the winds,
dance and twirl, sing to the sky, coves, caves, cliffs,
and three brothers watch them—for hours.

The eldest says, "Collect the sealskins and say,
    'I have your selkie skin and I claim you for my bride.'"
The first two call for their maids, then the youngest—
he's fallen for the selkie whose skin he won, cries:

"My love is greater than the oceans of the world,"
he claims her, watches his sweetheart yearning.
In his heart he sees the sorrows of the world
for she will always belong to those oceans.

The sealskins are secreted, locked away,
if the brides find them it's back to the water.
The young lad can't bear his selkie pining,
he yields her garment, and she returns to the sea.

The oldest lad's bride tracks down her sealskin.
But the middle boy burns his bride's seal pelt;

contd…

47

she rushes to save it and dies in the flames.
The flickering flames of the fire. He expires.

The youngest brother weeps on the seashore
praying his bride will return to his side.
She swims to the shoreline every ninth night,
cools on a conch shell, dances with him again.

Entanglement

'This is the one song that everyone
would like to learn: the song
that is irresistible'.
Margaret Attwood (1998)

Threads of melodies tack through sultry air,
weave over waves, surge past the shore,
travel to a boat and see the split shot sinkers
he presses onto lines to give them weight.

His head tilts like a vertical bobbin,
shuttles back and forth to pick up the thread,
wonders where the sound originates,
ponders—perhaps it's only in his head.

The sound's in the shape of his lover
the woman he dreams of through the day
and then he sees his line is entangled,
he won't make it back to her early this way.

He picks at the line and starts to unravel
yet siren threads drift closer, he hears
them become the soft tone
of his love's sweet blandishments,

'Promise you'll be early
tonight, my dear?'
He shakes his head, the song enthralls.
Home calls, his wish: to kiss her soon.

Leigh

Crumpled Sheets

Your sleep-loose arm is weighty on my back
and crumpled sheets surround our sweaty sheen:
sweet sugar spooning bodies, hot contact,
I rise before my morning state is seen.
I rinse my mouth and shower soft, and then
get back to you, maybe we start again?
You'll wash and shave the raucous night away,
pure loving tender selves will be restored,
but work calls now and when we join once more,
our tangled bed will evidence the day.

The Girl in the Chair and Her Protégé

She cups a small bird in her hand,
born this year, feathers silken, soft,
she encourages flight, holds it aloft,
so warm, so weak, it trembles.

She wheels her chair along smooth garden ways,
wishes there were more she could do, she prays.
A feather drops, makes her cough;
the bird stays in the hayloft.

She keeps the silence of the barn,
leaves the bird in its haven, whereon
the creature stills, mute and calm,
scented hay burns the air as a balm.

The gentle girl returns the next day,
no drama, the bird has flown away.
The girl in the chair and her protégé.

Odd Spoons

The move reveals a collection
of Ma's odd spoons.
One has a rose pattern
and tells of stainless steel,
how it doesn't need polishing,
will remain bright.
A silver spoon,
somewhat tarnished,
retorts that shininess,
like a nineteen-fifties actress,
comes cheap.

I still smell the unmistakeable fragrance
of Silvo with wadding,
as Ma taught me to polish;
newspaper spread before us,
yellow dusters with red edges.
Thanks to papers and cleaner
the dusters became black.

Apostle spoons; deep-bowled soupspoons;
a perforated absinthe spoon
with lacy wormwood leaves
that allows liquor to flow over a sugar cube,
the spoon notched to balance on the glass;
Ma never used that,
her face grew taut at the sight of it,
but I loved it in its diversity.

The Anton Michelsen Christmas spoon,
enamelled in blue, white and gold,
Ma used it to measure tea
it was lost long ago...
when Grandma moved out.   contd...

Egg spoons, salt, sugar, teaspoons,
dessert and grapefruit spoons; straight spoons
and gay spoons
sit beside the tablespoons,
as glorious as Eddie Izzard,
as colourful as Grayson Perry.
Not odd.
Each one celebrates its difference.

Summer Meadow

Time for dogs to stroll,
as sun beats through shade in cedar.
Beneath feet, tunnels mole
while insects follow-my-leader.

The dogs don't play the game,
they raise an eye, a brow,
'Don't care' they sniff, declaim,
'it's too hot anyhow.'

White umbels hum and hover,
alien crafts swoop, dip then tower
above grasses' itchy pother,
and burdock in full flower.

Rust green spires spring
over yellow tilted shades,
hear bombus choirs sing
above parasol parades.

Echoes heard,
warm summer words,
calls of birds,
dogs doze, droop, demur.

The Herring Girls | Gutted

The men pull on ropes, land the catch;
tug a trade more dangerous than mining.
Here come the herring girls on blue buses,
slumped on slatted wooden seats
click-clack knitting.
Click-clack ganseys[1] on the quay,
awaiting the catch.

Bind up your fingers,
gabby herring girls,
save yourselves from the slice
of lethal knives.
Wear wooden clogs for sure-footing,
fish scales make walking
a dangerous game, the slime...

Rows of herring boats line the quayside,
a busy fleet overfishing the seas.
Fishwives in stench,
odours that rise and never fall.
Nimble fingers fleet and fast,
packers and gutters
salt, basket and barrel the catch.
Gutters tip fish into farlans[2],
gut, drop into baskets,
the packer packs barrels layered with salt.

Steam billows, shrouds the women,
hair covered by gurcaidhs[3];
fisher lassies in pinnies,   contd…

---

[1] *Heavy fishermen's jumpers*
[2] *Long boxes or troughs*
[3] *Headbands or handkerchiefs tied over the hair*

overalls, aprons smeared with fish stink,
the gutting tables are frantic
as the morning wears out.
Tubs fill with foul-smelling waste.

Fast-fingered cleckin[1] women
work in all weathers,
wee loons[2] and quines[3] swarm,
play tag, slip shoeless, footed in filth.
Perks for fish workers; the Friday Fry.
Gutting, cleaning, putting away,
all for a pittance at the end of the day.
They eat well on a Friday night.

---

[1] *Gossiping mothers*
[2] *Boys*
[3] *Girls*

For Walls

Pardon those seeking refuge, as they are without blame,
we cannot know their history and they must have a home.
Let them return and return to their place of safety,
stay with the door closed on the world outside
wrapped in warm arms where everything looks right,
everything smells right, sheltered by bricks and mortar,
secure, connected, where lasting memories are made,
big laughs, biggest smiles, most love.
The walls of home shape mood, shape outlook on life,
pardon those seeking refuge, as they are without blame.

November | Heading for a Country Winter

a response to 'Country Summer' by Leonie Adams

In the hedgerows, haws are darkening,
part-abandoned by blackbirds,
they slur to carmine, beyond gems,
beyond melting rubies on the stark bones of May;
they will last over winter until buds return.
The trees are glad of lichen, stark and cold ochre-grey,
no innocence of green remains
and no lark's-bite berries to taste.
The low sun lurks, leers
when it deigns to appear.

Orion the hunter, bright in chill nights,
is easy to recognise
and followed by first frosts in early hours,
tickles of silver and itches of white
where the meadow grass rises, brown yet majestic.
The mowers are in the old barn.
Stray seeds cling and rattle on slender stalks,
defy the onset of the harshest season.
The rust-coated mare is stabled.
Dreams are no longer idle.

Midwinter Spindle

Morning
spikes the eye with frost;
the pink spindle
has never been
more beautiful,
less vain.

Abundant galanthus flowers
form a snowpaque blanket.
The spindle pivots
on dainty white petticoats,
shy milk flowers
skitter at its feet.

The Seasons Turn

The green-brown burrs of autumn have gone,
the beechnuts consumed or rotting
in the now-fallen foliage.
When people come
they'll walk a straight path,
see boulders lined shoulder-to-shoulder,
stroll beneath soon-to-be-bare frames
of slender trees.

In the avenue they'll be safe
if they take care.
Light, large-wheeled phaetons stay upright,
horses permitting,
but tip-tilting curricles must beware!
As they pass, the leaves swirl
before settling once more.

Artists arrive, all chatter and clatter,
paints, palettes and easels;
they point and name the colours:
oxblood red, sable brown, topaz, ochre, and charcoal
black;
hints of olive and pistachio green remain,
as if to be tasted.
While, hovering around the corridor of trees
amethyst tints imbued with light and shade
applaud as the scent of winter approaches.

These are the minutes,
all the wishfulness,
every heartfelt loss and glorious gain
of our times.
As many wishes as leaves on the ground,
thought of as often as the burrs of autumn.
And the seasons turn.

Acknowledgements

'Hobgoblin Trees' *Slants of Light* (Paragram Press 2013)

'What Ma Said' *Remember* (Paragram Press 2014)

'William's Footprint' *The Sole to Soul Project* (Croome Court 2014)

'A Minuet in Time' *The Sole to Soul Project* (Croome Court 2014)

'Candles and Splinters' *Spotlights* (Paragram Press 2015)

'Walk' *Pro-Saeculum* (Romania 2016)

'The Making' *Pro-Saeculum* (Romania 2016)

'Latent' *Slants of Light* (Paragram Press 2013) and *Pro-Saeculum* (Romania 2016)

'Tender Fruit' *Plum Lines* (Croome Court 2016) and *The Alchemy of 42* (Black Pear Press 2020)

'not sorry yet' *Girl's Got Rhythm* (Black Pear Press 2012 and 2016)

'Bittersweet' *Paradox* (Paragram Press 2016)

'If You Didn't Get This Message Call Me' *Paradox* (Paragram Press 2016)

'Swifts' *Openings 33* (OUP 2016) and *Pro-Saeculum* (Romania 2016)

'Farewell' *Paradox* (Paragram Press 2016)

'Spade', 'Bird on Spade', and 'Head Alone' all exhibited at *The Jinney Ring Craft Centre* 2017

'Pale Horse' *Contour Special Edition* © 2018

'Letter Writing in the Moonlight' *Contour Special Edition* © 2018

'Raw' *Poetry of Worcestershire* (Offa's Press 2019)

'The Vengeful Ghost' *The Alchemy of 42* (Black Pear Press 2020)

'For Walls' *One of the winning poems in The Worcester Amnesty International Competition* (2020)

'The Seasons Turn' *Dear Reader,* (2021) *https://ift.tt/3touyhK*

'Midwinter Spindle' *The Poetree Project—Winter* (2021)

Reviews

Polly Stretton's *Growing Places* is a wonderfully rich collection, ranging from family intimacies through to earthy encounters. Stretton draws from all manner of inspirations to pull readers in both emotionally and in more concrete ways, using imagery that roots us in specific times and places.

Insofar as the collection's title, growing places is indeed achieved here. We move through her recollections, countryside wanders, and life experiences in such a way that it is impossible not to feel these poems spring up around you and build their own worlds through your reading.

The work is lavish, evocative and utterly charming, and *Growing Places* is a collection worth setting aside some time for.

Charley Barnes—Worcestershire Poet Laureate 2019-2020—Writer in Residence, The Swan Theatre, Worcester—Managing Director Sabotage Reviews—Visiting Lecturer, and Editor Dear Reader

Growing Places—love the separation into places, Malvern, Croome and so on, it gives a good structure for the poems. I enjoyed the childhood/memory poems and others including 'Letter Writing in Moonlight', 'Pale Horse' and 'Latent'.

Amanda Bonnick—Worcester Cathedral Poet-in-Residence 2020

I appreciated the variety of subject, form and style. Polly is particularly skilled in creating a sense of time and place and the best poems have some stunningly original imagery. I especially liked 'Tender Fruit' and 'Flawless' and 'The Vengeful Ghost' flows like...a ghost.

Nigel Kent—Poet and Webmaster—Open University Poetry Society

Growing Places is a beautiful collection of place, some real, some imagined, and of identity. This work of reminiscence connecting memories of Worcestershire warms with pieces around Malvern, its Hills and Droitwich. Yet you need not have visited to appreciate the landscapes Polly evokes, so carefully are they crafted, so profoundly do those echoes resonate. What writer has not also indulged in fantasy place creation? A place where the protagonist can cut loose unfettered by temporal barriers. In this land without borders, Polly excels.

The Malvern sequence sees the town through the eyes of a child just embarking on her school career, a heady mix of youthful exuberance and parental struggle. 'What Ma Said', told almost as a nursery rhyme, is particularly poignant. And then to the Hills, where the playfulness of tumbling swifts can be heard as well as imagined.

Hitherto I had been unaware of the Kyrielle, a French form of rhyming poetry written in quatrains. With each quatrain containing a repeating line or phrase as a refrain, usually appearing as the last line of each stanza. Each line within the poem consists of only eight syllables. It requires great discipline, but comes with its rewards, as evidenced here in 'Beyond the Veil'.

A few of the poems have been published in periodicals before, this collection gathering together a diverse body of material united by sharp, concise writing, and genuine affection for its subjects. Gentle rhyme and unobtrusive alliteration an oft repeated hallmark of the content. Tucked away is a little gem, an Aubade 'Crumpled Sheets' in which erotica oozes from the page like the afterglow of lovers. This characterises the collection, just when you find comfort in a familiar theme, so Polly finds something to surprise, and delight.

Gary Longden—Staffordshire Poet Laureate 2014-2015 and a former writer in residence at Uttoxeter Racecourse